U.S. ★ WARPLANES
THE B-2 SPIRIT

E. E. Basmadjian

the rosen publishing group's
rosen central

Published in 2003 by The Rosen Publishing Group, Inc.
29 East 21st Street, New York, NY 10010

First Edition

Library of Congress Cataloging-in-Publication Data

Basmadjian, E. E.
The B-2 Spirit / by E.E. Basmadjian.— 1st ed.
    p. cm. — (U.S. warplanes)
Summary: Discusses the history of the B-2 Spirit stealth bomber and its use in the military campaigns in Afghanistan after the September 11, 2001, terrorist attacks.
Includes bibliographical references and index.
ISBN 0-8239-3869-7 (library binding)
1. B-2 bomber—Juvenile literature. [1. B-2 bomber. 2. Stealth aircraft. 3. Bombers.] I. Title. II. Series.
UG1242.B6 B373 2002
623.7'463—dc21
                                                                2002008482

Manufactured in the United States of America

CONTENTS

Underside view of a B-2A Spirit in flight. The use of special antiradar coatings and curvatures rather than flat surfaces means that this vast "flying wing" appears no bigger than a bird to all but the most powerful land-based radars.

"It doesn't have any wings. It is one."
—Anonymous employee who worked on the stealth bomber, 1967

May 2001. Whiteman Air Force Base (AFB), Missouri. Four B-2 stealth bomber pilots from the 509th Bomb Wing complete a fifty-hour combat mission in a flight simulator. Little did these pilots imagine that a few months later, their missions would be real ones, and that they would be playing an important role in a war against terrorism.

This is exactly what happened. On September 11, 2001, the attacks on New York City's World Trade Center and the Pentagon in Arlington, Virginia, rocked the world and led the United States to declare a "war against terror." This war pitted American and allied forces against the Al Qaeda terrorist group, which was responsible for the attacks, as well as against the man who founded

September 11, 2001: The south tower of the World Trade Center collapses. The north tower burns in the foreground, collapsing shortly afterward and spreading dust and debris throughout downtown Manhattan.

this group, Osama bin Laden. Osama bin Laden and other leaders of Al Qaeda were given refuge by Afghanistan's ruling Taliban, a group of Muslim extremists who had seized control of this central Asian nation five years earlier.

While supporting Osama bin Laden and his anti-American views, the Taliban governed the Afghan people with extreme harshness. All freedoms were suspended and many citizens were brought to the brink of starvation. Following the attacks, President George W. Bush vowed that all terrorists and supporters of terrorism would be punished for their crimes against humanity. In the first stage of this war—called Operation Enduring Freedom—the prime targets were Osama bin Laden, the members of Al Qaeda, and the Taliban. And the presence of B-2s would be crucial.

On October 7, six B-2 bombers, each with a pilot and copilot, took off from Whiteman Air Force Base. Their mission—to fly halfway around the world and hit ground targets in Afghanistan—would take them forty-four hours. Not only would this be the longest combat mission in the history of aviation, but it would also usher in a new age in modern warfare. For the first time, the U.S. Air Force had a bomber that combined long range, a large payload (bombs and missiles), near-precision weapons, and stealth—all in one fantastic aircraft. Its special talents would pave the way to military success.

1 A NEW AGE IN MODERN WARFARE

On October 7, 2001, American aircraft began bombing targets in Afghanistan. These targets included airfields and air defense sites, fuel depots, military bases, and hideouts of the Al Qaeda organization. The strikes were carefully planned to avoid hitting Afghan citizens. They were so successful that three days later, most Taliban air defenses had been destroyed and U.S. forces were in control of the skies over Afghanistan.

The B-2 had a major role in this early military success. This chapter will examine the special features that make this bomber so revolutionary and efficient.

Home in Time for Dinner

This B-2 drops a B61-11 bomb casing. Nicknamed "the bunker buster," the B61-11 is a tactical nuclear weapon designed to attack enemy bunkers hidden deep underground.

Traditionally, large numbers of military personnel and equipment deployed from many locations were necessary to wage an attack in enemy territory. Planes couldn't just take off from U.S. bases, fly around the world, drop their bombs, and fly home. They had to make stops to refuel, change pilots, and load weapons. To do this, they relied

Brigadier General Tony Przybyslawski stands proudly in front of a B-2 that has returned after a forty-four-hour bombing mission in Afghanistan, the longest air combat mission in military history. General Przybyslawski noted that people, not planes, are key to the success of the bombing missions in Afghanistan, saying that "We have America's best [people] flying, maintaining, and supporting this aircraft. I couldn't be prouder of these people."

on air bases in American territories or allied countries, as well as navy aircraft carriers that functioned as floating airports. These stops were time-consuming.

The B-2 changed all the rules with its incredibly long range. This remarkable bomber can fly more than 7,595 miles (12,223 kilometers) without refueling. It can fly over 11,000 miles (17,700 kilometers) with just one refueling. And even when the B-2 needs to refuel, it does so in the air.

In a thirty- to forty-hour mission, a B-2 pilot can take off from Whiteman Air Force Base, go straight to a conflict zone, drop his payload, and return to Missouri in time to eat dinner. As Brigadier General Anthony Przybyslawski, commander of the 509th Bomb Wing—the only squadron in the United States that flies the B-2s—told *Air Force Magazine*: "Now, when a pilot finishes his mission, he has to go home and cut the grass . . . It's an amazing statement in technology."

STEALTH

The B-2 is a stealth bomber, and its "stealthiness" is what makes it the most enduring aircraft in the world. These days, a bomber has to be able to fly into enemy airspace—without help from support aircraft—and destroy its most valued and heavily defended targets in the first crucial hours or days of a war. Although speed, precision, and long range are essential, even more important is the element of surprise.

The B-2 defeats an enemy's radar systems using sophisticated stealth technologies. Although it isn't quite invisible, the bomber possesses a number of low observable (LO) features. These features make it next to impossible for even advanced defense systems to detect, track, and attack the B-2. These stealth features include the materials used to build the plane, its special coatings, its flying wing design, and its "silent" engines. Many other stealth features remain top secret.

As a pilot who has spent over 100 hours flying the B-2, General Przybyslawski is proud to be the officer in charge of the B-2 squadron. The 509th Bomb Wing's "home" is Whiteman AFB in Johnson County, Missouri. Whiteman is also "home" to twenty combat-ready B-2s and additional planes used for training.

Large Payloads

Another striking feature of the B-2 is its large payload. Over 40,000 pounds (18,144 kilograms, or kg) to be precise. Just two bombers with four pilots can deliver thirty-two precision-guided 2,000-pound (907-kg) bombs. Before the B-2 came along, such a mission would have required sixteen F-117 fighters, four tankers, and many more crewmembers. The B-2 can carry both nuclear and conventional weapons. Conventional weapons can range from Mk-84 500-pound (227-kg) bombs and sea mines to 2,000-pound (907.2-kg) precision-guided weapons.

In 1999, the B-2 was the first aircraft ever to use the satellite-guided Joint Direct Attack Munition (JDAM) bomb. The following year, in 2000,

Grounded for the moment in its Missouri hangar, the *Spirit of Mississippi* gets ready for another long mission. The B-2 can fly with over 40,000 pounds (18,144 kilograms) of both nuclear and conventional weapons, an impressive feat considering that it will carry its heavy payload halfway around the world and back without having to land in order to refuel.

the B-2 also began using the satellite-guided Joint Standoff Weapon (JSOW). These weapons are known as smart bombs. This is because instead of just being dropped, they are fed information by computers that steer them automatically to their targets. This makes them incredibly precise.

Precision

Extreme precision is another of the B-2's talents. In March 1999, B-2s went to battle for the first time in the former Republic of Yugoslavia. During this mission, 90 percent of the bombs dropped by B-2s fell within forty feet (twelve meters) of their targets.

"The B-2s go out there and carry sixteen very precise munitions," said Brigadier General Leroy Barnidge Jr., former commander of the

509th Bomb Wing, in an interview with *Air Force Magazine*. "We can take this thing thousands of miles; we can go into very lethal environments, and we can put the bombs exactly where we want them. Then we bring the guys home, turn the jets and do it again. That's not a bad return on your investment."

The B-2's precision is an invaluable asset, permitting the bomber to quickly take out key military and communications (telephone, radio, and radar) targets. This leaves an enemy "deaf," "blind," and unable to fight back. For this reason, B-2s are often sent to bomb airfield runways. Undetected from thousands of feet above, a single B-2 can destroy two airfields in a single mission. Unable to take off because of the bombed-out craters on the runways, enemy warplanes are stranded. They become easy targets for other nonstealthy bombers, such as B-52s, which come to finish the job by dropping large numbers of unguided, or "dumb," bombs.

BULL'S EYE

The B-2 needs to deliver its payload with speed and accuracy. To do this, it depends on a unique targeting system called the GPS-Aided Targeting System (GATS). GPS stands for global positioning system: a network of twelve satellites that revolve around Earth.

As they get close to a target, the pilots use the B-2's radar system to take two radar snapshots of the target and the area around it. The first picture shows the aimpoints. The second gives the pilots information about the plane's distance to the target. Using the GATS, the B-2's computer compares both pictures and calculates the exact moment at which the bomb should be released. The computer also sends information about the aimpoints to each guided, or smart, bomb. Bombs are attached to the computer by an electronic umbilical cord. In effect, the computer "talks" to the bombs. Once the bombs are released from the bomb bay door, they continue to receive information from the satellites that steer them to their target. Because of this system, the B-2's weapons always hit their targets.

THE WORLD'S STEALTHIEST BOMBER

"Those watching the barely visible B-2 during a takeoff on that January day gasped when the wafer-thin bomber lifted off and then rolled into a sharp bank, suddenly revealing the vast sweep and size of the black wing. Even more shocking was the quietness of its four F118 19,000 pound [8,614 kg] thrust engines as they propelled the aircraft into the sky. Normally, the roar of the jet engines would have been ear-shattering, easily heard miles away. The sound of the B-2, however, could almost be called unobtrusive."

—Description of the inaugural flight of *Spirit of Missouri*, the first B-2 to take off in January 1994 from Whiteman AFB. (published in *Air Force Magazine*).

More than anything else, it is the B-2's stealth—the ability to go undetected and take the enemy by surprise—that makes it such an amazing aircraft. Stealth is one of the most important tactics when trying to win a war. However, with tracking radar that is more sensitive than ever, and with missiles able to chase down planes from hundreds of miles away, how does one avoid detection?

The designers of the B-2 stealth bomber had a real challenge on their hands. Their biggest problem was how to take a plane whose wings stretch wider than half a football field and make its presence on a radar screen similar to that of a small bird flying in the sky.

A Flying Wing

The B-2's most obvious stealth feature is its design. In photos, the B-2 resembles a bat. In fact, engineer John Northrop's design is based on a "flying wing." Because it has no vertical surfaces, pilots have nicknamed the paper-thin aircraft a "flying pencil" or a "hyphen." Its flatness, along with its curved surfaces (it has no sharp angles—even the wings end in curves), make it difficult to pick up on a radar screen.

With this design, and the plane's coating of reflective paint, radar that hits the aircraft is bounced away from the B-2 in many directions. Because there is no signal that returns to the enemy's radar station, the B-2 is basically invisible.

There are other advantages to the flying wing design. Its flatness means less resistance from air and heavy winds. This allows the plane to fly at higher speeds and carry larger loads for longer distances and at greater heights. Furthermore, instead of being stored within a narrow fuselage—a plane's central section, where passengers and cargo are held—the payload can be evenly distributed, allowing for greater balance and stability.

A Special Skin

Every surface, every edge, and every screw of the B-2 is coated in special reflective black paint and tape. With this smooth "skin," the B-2, like a bat, can fly camouflaged into the night. The skin also scatters radar signals. And while most planes are made out of aluminum, the B-2 is built with graphite, which absorbs and traps signals inside the plane, thereby distorting radar readings.

The B-2's shape, coupled with its lightweight carbon-based structure, makes it naturally very light and efficient. These factors allow the B-2 to run on lower power settings that make very little noise. Also, because its four engines are located deep inside the plane, the noise is muffled.

Tightening Up

Although the B-2's pilots need to communicate, many radio and radar signals can be detected by enemy radar. Because of this, it is

KEEPING COOL

One of the biggest threats to war planes are heat-seeking missiles. These missiles are drawn to a plane by the heat its engines give off. The B-2 keeps missiles away by having its heat-generating engines located inside the plane. It is also equipped with special jets that cool the exhaust before the exhaust flows outside. As an extra safety measure, exhaust is released from the top of the plane, instead of from the bottom, as is usually the case. This makes it harder for low-flying aircraft with infrared tracking devices to detect the B-2.

necessary to take certain precautions to keep the enemy from intercepting signals. For example, instead of using a wide radar signal, the B-2 uses synthetic aperture radar, which has a smaller signal. For similar reasons, pilots keep radio transmissions to a minimum. Lastly, because the design resembles a watertight vessel, the B-2 doesn't "leak" electromagnetic signals that might be picked up by enemy radar systems.

The B-2 is most vulnerable to detection when its bomb doors open to drop a bomb. "The doors are open three to five seconds," said Lieutenant Colonel Tony Imondi, one of the B-2's qualified instructor pilots, in an interview published in *Air Force Magazine*. "There is no way they're going to lock us up and shoot us down in three to five seconds. The endgame takes a whole lot longer than that. That's the whole paradigm of stealth. It's not that they can't see you . . . They can't get you."

Although the B-2 is not totally invisible to radar, enemy radar needs to do more than just detect a B-2 in order to be able to destroy it. Air force experts admit that some very high-powered, land-based, long-range radar systems are capable of detecting the B-2—but without much precision. This lack of precision makes it virtually impossible to track the B-2 over a long distance, guide a missile to it, and have the missile actually hit the B-2.

Two F-117 Nighthawks escort a B-2 on a bombing mission. Although the B-2 can fly missions alone, the air force takes extra steps to make sure that nothing happens to their stealthy bombers. The F-117's unique shape also makes it difficult to observe by radar, and the aircraft was used frequently in Operation Desert Storm. Like all stealth planes, the B-2s and the F-117s will wait until dark to attack their target.

VITAL STATISTICS

Prime Contractor: Northrop Grumman Corporation

Length: 69 feet (21.03 meters)

Height: 17 feet (5.18 meters)

Wingspan: 172 feet (52.43 meters)

Speed: High subsonic, 475 miles per hour (1,010 kilometers per hour)

Maximum Altitude: Over 55,000 feet (16,765 meters)

Maximum Range: 6,600 miles, or 10,620 kilometers, (with 24,000-pound, or 108,864-kilogram, payload)

Engines: 4 General Electric F118-GE-100 turbofans

Thrust: 19,000 pounds (8,618 kilograms) each engine

Building a B-2

Hundreds of new manufacturing techniques had to be "discovered" to construct the B-2. For example, many of the materials used to make its parts are made of composite materials that mix carbon, glass fibers, and resins. In fact, more than 10,000 composite materials were created just for the B-2. And aside from actual materials, entirely new systems were invented to build the B-2. These range from robotic drills to ultrasonic cutters. Many of the systems developed for the B-2 are still guarded as secrets by the companies that invented them, or are considered classified information by the government.

Maintenance

Although the B-2 is a complex aircraft, keeping it in perfect condition is actually quite easy. This is because instead of a mechanic having to

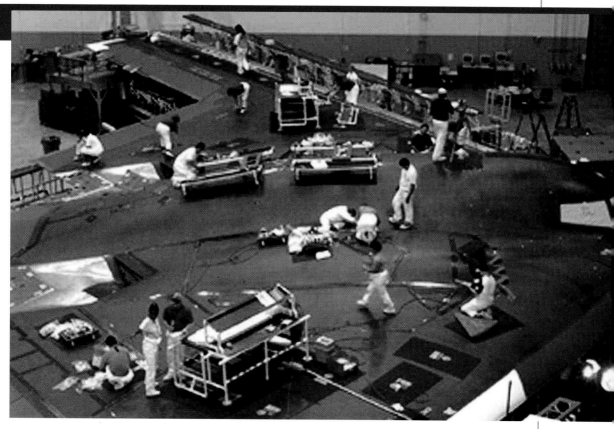

At Whiteman AFB, the maintenance crew of this B-2 bomber works hard to get it ready for a flight (or mission). All bumps and scratches on its skin are sanded and repainted.

search for the exact cause or location of a problem, the plane itself is able to detect when something is wrong with it. It can even fix the problem itself.

How does this process work? Each electrical or mechanical part of the B-2 is equipped with a Reference Designated Indicator (RDI). When the part malfunctions, a message is automatically sent to the plane's flight-control computer and printed on the maintenance printer. The computer is programmed to diagnose even the smallest of glitches. Searching through all of its memory banks, the computer "talks" to itself and often automatically makes corrections on its own. If a problem occurs in flight, the plane "tells" the pilot about it.

One of the most difficult parts of the B-2 to maintain is its special "skin." The natural damage that occurs to any plane traveling 545 miles per hour (1,010 kilometers per hour) in heavy rain or hail can bang up the B-2's smooth skin, which is key to its invisibility. After each flight, a technician wearing special soft-soled shoes carefully examines 10,000 square feet (3,048 square meters) of plane surface for nicks, scratches, and peeling paint. Special methods have been developed to patch the scratched or damaged skin.

Maintenance is carried out in a windowless hangar at the base. Common problems are cracks in the special coating or the peeling off of reflective tape. As maintenance supervisor Captain Casey W. Hughson told *Air Force Magazine*, "Tape is tape. Fly [the B-2] around long enough at high speed and it will start to peel back." As such, tape must be carefully and perfectly reapplied. Even the tiniest bump on the surface can considerably increase the plane's chances of being detected by enemy radar. "What these guys do isn't a science; it's an art," says Captain Hughson of the plane's maintenance technicians. "For example, getting the paint on exactly one [millimeter] thick—that's an art."

Says Lieutenant Colonel Tony Imondi, "You don't go out and turn a wrench on a stealth airplane without thinking, 'What's the impact if I scratch this thing?' because there is an impact."

The search for a stealthy plane began over sixty years ago. During World War II, radar was used for the first time to detect attacking fleets of enemy aircraft. To avoid detection, engineers considered how to make planes that would be more difficult to track. One of the designs they came up with was a plane that was essentially one enormous wing. The great advantage of this design was the reduction of the number of angles off which radar signals could bounce. The problem was that a plane without regular wings and a tail to stabilize the craft would yaw, or deviate wildly, veering to the right and to the left of its flight path.

In 1943, two German brothers, Walter and Reimer Horten, were the first to come up with a working model of such a plane. Their twin-engine flying wing bomber was made out of two layers of plywood with a core of sawdust, glue, and charcoal. The charcoal was used to absorb radar waves. Since the war was still being fought, however, Germany had little money to spend on experimental airplanes.

Northrop's Flying Wing

The next person to try building the perfect wing was American aircraft designer John Northrop. Northrop had been experimenting with a flying wing design since the 1920s. But it was only in 1946 that the Northrop Aircraft Company's XB-35 bomber made its appearance. Plagued with engine and gearbox problems, the design was adapted for jet power and, in 1947, the eight-jet YB-49 took to the air.

As the big plane flew around the country, a strange phenomenon became apparent: The new plane was often difficult to see in the air, and under some conditions, it almost completely disappeared from radar screens. The U.S. government was interested in purchasing the

John K. Northrop rests his hand on the "flying wing," the very first attempt at building a stealth airplane. Although it might seem unlikely, the plane you see here would eventually grow into the B-2. Northrop attempted to adapt his flying wing design to a number of different kinds of aircraft, ranging from war planes to eighty-seat passenger transports. Unfortunately, not all of these designs made it off the testing ground, or even off the drawing board.

plane, but changed its mind when test runs revealed that the aircraft was slow and unstable.

Throughout the 1950s and 1960s, researchers kept searching for ways to make planes invisible. Rubber-based radar absorbers used on U-2 spy planes proved unsuccessful. More promising was Lockheed's SR-71, an all-black bomber with slanted surfaces that became known as the first stealth airplane.

Dreams of a stealth plane remained on the back burner until the late 1970s. In 1978, Americans were taken hostage in Iran. And in 1979, the former Soviet Union's invasion of Afghanistan increased tensions between the United States and the USSR. Amid this charged political climate, the creation of a fleet of stealthy bombers became a priority, and U.S. president Jimmy Carter authorized development of the ATB (Advanced Technology Bomber) program. Two aeronautical giants, Northrop and Lockheed, went head to head, each trying to outdo the other in coming up with a winning design that the government would approve.

At that time, stealth technology was somewhat of a mystery. Creating a stealth plane was seen as a feat of magic rather than as a product of science and engineering. And Lockheed was seen as the only company that knew the necessary magic tricks. In the end, though, Lockheed's proposed design, with the code name Senior Peg, proved less promising than that of Northrop.

The immediate forerunner to the B-2 was the Tacit Blue aircraft. It was created to fly unseen by radar near the front line of a ground battle, in order to monitor enemy locations and send information to a ground commander.

After forty years, Northrop had decided to resurrect the flying wing that had proved a failure in 1947. Now, however, computers could be used to control the plane's movements and bombing accuracy. Aided by this new technology, Northrop submitted a design code-named Senior Ice. In October 1981, the company won the contract to develop the B-2. However, nobody knew what a B-2 was or what it looked like. The designs and the project itself were a tightly guarded secret. There was a brief public announcement about Northrop winning the contract. Then, for the next seven years, nothing more was heard about this top-secret project, now code-named Senior CJ after the Pentagon's program office secretary, Connie Jo Kelly.

SEE HOW IT FLIES

Computers are the reason the B-2 doesn't yaw all over the place. The B-2 "flies by wire"—meaning that pilots navigate using the plane's computers (four of them) instead of the controls themselves. Every time the pilot inputs a control command, the four computers "vote" on the result it will have. For the command to be adopted, at least three computers must agree. Any mistake is automatically thrown out. Moreover, it is a computer that makes automatic adjustments when heavy winds or turbulence threaten to turn, pitch, or veer the plane from its course.

The best thing about this system is that all sorts of conditions and corrections can be programmed into the computers. For example, when the B-2's bomb doors are opened, an enormous amount of drag is created from air resistance: When a heavy bomb is dropped, the suddenly light plane will want to jump. Luckily, the computerized flight controls are programmed to automatically correct in advance both of these effects. All the pilot has to do is keep steering. The system is so efficient that, in theory, the computerized automatic pilot could actually fly an entire mission, from takeoff to landing, on its own. The only thing a human pilot would need to do is to give the proper power settings.

Twenty-One Planes

Originally, the government ordered 132 planes to be built. However, the collapse of the Soviet Union in the late 1980s brought an end to the possible threat of military conflict between the two nations. There was also the high cost of the planes—$44 billion—that many viewed as a waste of money.

To date, only twenty-one planes have been built. This is the number of B-2s in existence today. Each plane has a price tag of between $2.1 and $2.2 billion. Those who defend the high cost point out that the B-2's unique attributes and requirements make it very expensive to construct and keep in perfect working condition. However, critics have charged that such a fortune was spent only because the B-2 program was kept secret not only from the public, but from Congress as well.

Because the designs were top secret, it wasn't until November 1988, when the first prototype was revealed, that the B-2 was seen

November 22, 1988: The first B-2 Spirit is unveiled at Air Force Plant 42 in secluded Palmdale, California. On hand are members of the press and various military personnel. However, the B-2 would not be flown until July 17, 1989.

for the first time. It wasn't until July 17, 1989, that the first of six B-2 prototypes made its maiden flight. And it was only at the end of 1993 that the U.S. Air Force received its first aircraft.

Delivered to the 509th Bomb Wing at Whiteman AFB, the aircraft was baptized the *Spirit of Missouri* in honor of its new home. By the time it had arrived, it had completed 20,000 hours of fatigue testing at Edwards Air Force Base in California. In February 1994, the aircraft was officially named *Spirit*, although at Whiteman it is simply called "the jet." Subsequent B-2s, all named after states, took up residence at Whiteman. The last of the fleet of twenty-one planes, named *Spirit of America*, was delivered in July 2000.

The basic B-2 test program at Edwards AFB was completed on July 1, 1997. The total number of tests had taken eight years and 5,000 hours. However, it wasn't until 1999 that the B-2 went to war for the first time.

The B-2 Goes to War

The B-2 Spirit made its operational debut on March 24, 1999, participating in the first combat missions of Operation Allied Force

President Bill Clinton shakes hands with the pilots and crewmen who flew missions over Kosovo. The United States's portion of the NATO mission was called Noble Anvil, and it called for the careful bombing of key Serbian military targets. Clinton credited the B-2 pilots as the force behind making Slobodon Milosovic accept NATO's terms for peace.

against Serbian aggression in Kosovo. Two B-2s successfully dropped thirty-two 2,000-pound (907-kilogram) JDAM satellite-guided bombs on targets in the former Republic of Yugoslavia. The nonstop mission took thirty-one hours and proved that the B-2 was indeed the stealthiest of warplanes.

The conflict in Kosovo lasted seventy-two days. By the end, fifty-one pilots had flown the B-2. Most flew one mission; several flew two, and one pilot flew three times. Although it only flew in 1 percent of all missions, the stealth bomber was responsible for hitting 11 percent of all targets during the entire Kosovo conflict.

Despite years of criticism that its stealth and flight systems were too finicky and fragile for real combat, in Operation Allied Force the B-2 proved that it could fly halfway around the world, cause serious damage, and return home to Missouri without a scratch.

4 ON THE GROUND AND IN THE AIR

To many, it was fitting that the B-2 would go to the air force's 509th Bomb Wing, one of the most famous air units in American history. The 509th has existed since December 1944. It was created with a mission in mind: to drop the new, top-secret atomic bomb on a Japanese target.

Today the mission of the 509th's leaders is to instill in pilots and maintenance personnel a "stealth mindset." As such, the 509th is made up of a select group of highly experienced pilots who prepare other aviators to use the B-2s. It also includes a highly qualified ground crew. Many of the pilots and ground crew have been with the B-2 program since its creation in the early 1980s. Some officers remember being sent off to California years ago to work with Northrop personnel on a secret project about which they knew nothing. For years, they couldn't tell anybody what they were doing.

Waving from the window of his cockpit, Colonel Paul W. Tibbets of the 509th Composite Group prepares for takeoff in the *Enola Gay*, the plane that dropped the atomic bomb on Hiroshima, Japan.

To get to fly a B-2, pilots must go through a careful selection process. A candidate's record must be perfect, with no history of safety infractions. Each candidate needs the recommendation of a wing commander, as well as other recommendations and 1,000 hours of flight time. Many pilots have combat experience. Most have flown in bomber units, while others have flown fighter aircraft.

Training Day

New B-2 pilots are trained by air force instructor pilots. The training program is six months long. The first three months are spent in the classroom and in simulators that re-create the inside of a B-2's cockpit. The last three months of training are spent flying. Even once the first six months have passed, pilots continue to train over and over again.

Aside from flying the airplane and learning all about how it flies, pilots are involved in developing tactics for the airplane. This means learning how to operate the plane in order to get the maximum effect from its long range, payload, and stealth.

As Major Steve Tippets, an officer who took the B-2 training course, said in an issue of *Air Force Magazine*, "You come out of a simulator mission, after three or four hours, and you really feel as if you've flown the aircraft. You feel the same elation and fatigue, depending on how difficult the flying is."

Pilots flying simulator missions are monitored by instructors in another room. Instructors see everything the pilots see because every move they make and every button they push is electronically recorded. After a mission, pilots can study their every action. This information is kept in the pilots' training files. These files not only show pilots' progress over time, but also help to update the training program itself. If many pilots experience the same difficulties, there could be a problem with the way a procedure is being taught.

Having the same software in the Weapon System Trainer (WST) as in the B-2 allows pilots to rehearse missions before flying the aircraft. As Lieutenant Colonel Walter Denne, operations and training director of the B-2 Site Activation Task Force, told *Air Force Magazine*, "We can take mission data and . . . actually plug the mission into the simulator. So when a crew comes in to fly the simulator, they'll actually be flying

PRACTICE MAKES PERFECT—SIMULATION

A key part of the B-2 program is its simulators. Because there are only twenty-one B-2s in existence, the 509th depends on simulators more than actual planes for training. Pilots often spend thousands of hours training in simulators that allow them to learn everything—on the ground—about flying a B-2.

Three kinds of simulators are used for training: the Cockpit Procedures Trainer (CPT), Mission Trainer (MT), and Weapon System Trainer (WST).

★ The CPT gives pilots a feel for where switches are located in the plane and what they do. If a student hits the wrong switch, the system freezes. This ensures that pilots don't learn incorrect procedures.

★ The MT is a miniature WST that simulates the mission commander's right seat.

★ The WST is a full-motion simulator that is 95 to 98 percent similar to flying a real B-2. In fact, training inside a WST is almost exactly like handling a fully operational bomber. The WST compartment is an exact copy of the B-2's cockpit, and the computer software is exactly the same. Air pumps rock the seats, simulating turbulence or a rough landing. As well, a sophisticated graphics system recreates the countryside around Whiteman AFB, down to every tree within a 200-mile (322-kilometer) radius.

the real mission as planned for the next day. And mission rehearsal is where we pick up an awful lot of invaluable training because we can simulate hostile territory."

In the Air

Every B-2 pilot can count on flying about one sortie, or mission, a week. Each flight is preceded by a day of mission planning and a full "dress rehearsal" in the WST. Mission planning involves plotting radar threats the B-2 would face during a real mission and figuring out how to avoid or overcome them using the B-2's stealth capabilities. Planning takes place in a secure area where pilots have access to a database with information about various countries' air defenses.

As we learned earlier, the B-2 is flown by two pilots. The pilot in the left-hand seat actually flies the plane. Meanwhile, the pilot in the right-hand seat carries out the military mission. Responsible for navigation and bombing, this pilot can fly the plane as well. Because the B-2 is so highly automated, with computers doing so many tasks, one pilot can often take a nap while the other flies the airplane.

For general practice missions, pilots often fly to bombing ranges in Utah, Wisconsin, and Kansas. For very specific missions, they might rehearse at sites around the world. For general practice, usually one out of every five sorties involves the release of a live bomb, an inert bomb, or a smoke bomb. Otherwise, a weapon release can be fully simulated without any weapon actually being dropped.

Preparing for a Mission

In 1999, when NATO decided that it might have to use force against Serbia, the 509th began practicing for what would be its first combat mission. Fixed targets in the region had already been identified. These targets were programmed into the B-2's simulators. Pilots rehearsed strikes over and over again on the simulator before taking to the air.

Mission planning is done over several days in various steps:

★ **The Target** Four days before takeoff, pilots receive GPS coordinates of a target, along with images of the target area. All these are checked against radar images taken just before weapons release.

★ **The Flight Plan** The flight plan includes details about when and where to refuel, how to fly through defenses to the target area, and when to drop the bombs on the target.

Captain Greg Smith talks to a photographer inside the B-2 cockpit. The U.S. Air Force usually keeps its advanced planes under wraps, but they allowed the press to examine the B-2 after rumors spread that it was not effective.

★ **Familiarization** Pilots learn everything they can about conditions in the target area, in this case Yugoslavia, from the weather to the combat situation.

★ **Getting into Phase** Since all operations—takeoffs and the dropping of bombs—take place at night, pilots have to get into phase for a mission. They begin by sleeping during the day and staying awake at night. Getting into phase can also include getting extra sleep or avoiding distractions by staying in quarters usually reserved for visiting officers. Over time, each pilot has been trained to deal with long missions. Each pilot has a program tailored to his individual needs that takes into account diet, sleep, and other factors.

★ **Simulation** Pilots practice every aspect of a mission's combat phase several times. Since a B-2 only spends an hour or two in enemy airspace, attacks can be simulated over and over again.

STAYING AWAKE

Traveling around the world to drop bombs and returning home—all in one non-stop forty-to-fifty hour flight—is tiring to say the least. "For the initial round of combat, adrenaline alone will keep you going," says B-2 pilot Major Gregory A. Biscone. "The hard part is the return trip."

The B-2's cockpit is the size of that of a commercial jet, complete with a chemical toilet. Pilots learn to relax when not at the controls. Some nap on bed rolls that they can stretch out. Others read or do exercises in their seats.

Tests have proven the value of a twenty-to-thirty-minute "power nap." Such naps are easier to wake from than three-to-four-hour naps in which pilots fall into a deep sleep. Each pilot knows beforehand exactly how long he needs to sleep. If power naps are either too long or too short, the pilot will wake up feeling groggy.

Once the mission begins, pilots are not able to leave the simulator. Everything they require for a real mission has to be in the WST with them. Helmets, ejection seat harnesses, maps, food, water, and sleeping bags are packed into the cramped 10-foot by 10-foot (3.05-meter by 3.05-meter) full-motion B-2 cockpit simulator. A lounge chair for sleeping and a chemical toilet are also used.

Flying a Mission

An actual mission begins with final mission planning and inspection of the B-2s going into action. These tasks are carried out by other crewmembers. The pilots themselves rest and relax until takeoff. During this time, they can't be disturbed.

Even if they are heading for targets in entirely different regions, the B-2s taking off on the same night usually fly together from Whiteman AFB to support each other during the long trip. While in the air, planes refuel, often more than once. During the flight, pilots go over checklists of tasks, study images of their targets, stay tuned

THE LONGEST FLIGHT SIMULATOR

In May 2001, four pilots carried out the longest B-2 simulator mission in history: a fifty-hour flight in the B-2 WST.

The simulator mission was based on real-world targets and threats. The pilots "flew" from Whiteman, refueled in-flight six times, bombed targets, and landed at an overseas base.

Once the mission began, pilots could not leave the simulator. Everything they required for a real mission had to be in the WST with them. Helmets, ejection seat harnesses, maps, food, water, and sleeping bags were packed into the cramped 10-foot by 10-foot (3.05-meter by 3.05-meter) full-motion B-2 cockpit simulator. A lounge chair for sleeping and a chemical toilet were also used.

to changes in weather, and make sure every part of the plane is working. They sleep in shifts, taking power naps.

When they enter enemy territory, the pilots prepare for combat. They put on flight jackets, survival vests, and other necessary gear before powering up weapons and making sure that the computer is communicating with the bombs.

As they approach the target area, the GATS allows the B-2 mission commander to choose where the target will be hit. When the plane is close to the chosen target, the bomb bay doors open. A JDAM or JSOW weapon is released and steered to the target. Once out of the combat zone, the B-2s return home to Whiteman. On the ground, they "get back into line" and wait their turn to fly another mission.

MISSION
COMMANDER
GEN RYAN

PILOT
LT GEN MARCOTTE

DCC
SSGT M. THOMAS
ADCC
SRA B. MCDERMOTT

5 LOOKING INTO THE FUTURE

To Brigadier General Ronald C. Marcotte, being head of the B-2 program at Whiteman was the best job of his career. When asked in an issue of *Air Force Magazine* what lay ahead for the B-2, he replied that he couldn't see "the bomber losing its place in the near future."

The B-2 offers "a tremendous advantage because it ensures the capability to slow down an enemy," he said. To date, technological improvements in engines and weapons for smaller planes haven't come close to matching the B-2's ability to "get a warning order and twenty hours later be dropping bombs" precisely on target.

The B-2's successful performance in Kosovo and Afghanistan means the aircraft won't be retiring anytime soon. However, it is also unlikely that the government will be ordering more of the costly planes. Aside from the high price tags, the stealth bomber's overly sensitive skin—which requires high maintenance after almost every mission—is a problem. Furthermore, its current "low observability" is likely to become "high observability" as enemy radar systems become more sensitive.

It is likely that the stealth bomber will receive a technological makeover that will make it even more efficient and accurate. The following are some of the upgrades being planned for the B-2 in the near future:

★ Link 16

Link 16 is a system that offers secure digital sharing of data between different aircraft and between aircraft and other American and allied military services. Features of the system include real-time pictures of targets and combat areas, quick sharing of information, and the ability to change targets on short notice. Link 16 will make mission planning—especially once a plane is in the air—easier and more accurate.

★ EHF Satellite Communications System

The U.S. Air Force plans to develop an extremely high frequency (EHF) satellite communications system that will make it much easier for the B-2 to control and send commands to its weapons.

★ Digital Engine Controllers

The B-2 currently possesses a type of engine controller that has a high rate of failure. Replacing these problematic controllers with high-tech digital ones will improve the plane's performance, making it more reliable and easier to maintain.

★ Computers

As computer technology advances and more demands are placed on the aircraft systems, the B-2's increasingly outdated computers will need to be replaced with more sophisticated processors. Although the current computers are reliable, maintenance is increasingly complicated and expensive.

★ Stealth Improvements

Although the B-2 is currently nearly invisible to enemy radar systems, the bomber's stealthiness is bound to decrease over time. New materials and technologies will be necessary to maintain its low observability.

★ Smaller, More Precise Bombs—and More of Them

According to U.S. Air Force reports cited in *Air Force Magazine*, the next generation of precision-guided weapons will emphasize "longer range to minimize crew risk; miniaturization to enable more kills per sortie; and increased accuracy to ensure destruction with a smaller weapon and to minimize the chances for collateral damage."

The Joint Direct Attack Munition (JDAM) is a kit that takes normal missiles and turns them into smart weapons. A target's coordinates can be entered before the B-2 takes off, so that the payload can be launched once the aircraft gets within striking range. This photo shows a cluster of JDAM-guided missiles on a B-52 Stratofortress.

Greater precision in a smaller bomb means that each bomber on a single mission can hit more targets—possibly as many as eighty-four. Currently, a 2,000-pound (907-kilogram) JDAM is required for a single target. This is to make sure that if the bomb falls at some distance from the bull's-eye, the explosion will be powerful enough to hit the target. A more precise guided weapon than the JDAM, such as the AGM-154 JSOW (Joint Standoff Weapon), and the new JASSM (Joint Air-to-Surface Standoff Missile, a guided long-range missile similar to the JSOW bomb)— would require a smaller explosion and thus a smaller bomb.

Life of a B-2

When the B-2 was first being tested, calculations were made to see how long a "useful" life it would have. Test results showed that the average B-2 would be able to rack up approximately 40,000 flight hours before it would need to be retired due to wear and tear. According to a rough estimate, this means that one B-2 will go out of commission every ten years. Since the minimum number of aircraft required to make up the B-2 force is nineteen planes, with a fleet of only twenty-one B-2A Spirits, this means that by 2027 the B-2 force could be extinct.

GLOSSARY

aimpoint A mark or target.

allies Nations that join in battle.

Al Qaeda An anti-American terrorist group founded and led by Osama bin Laden. Al Qaeda was responsible for the September 11, 2001, terrorist attacks on the United States.

composite material Material made of two or more different substances.

conventional weapons Bombs or missiles that are not nuclear.

extremists People who have extreme or exaggerated beliefs.

fuselage The central portion of a plane in which passengers and cargo are located.

global positioning system (GPS) A system that uses satellites to accurately locate specific targets. Also frequently used by civilians.

infraction A violation.

Joint Attact Direct Munition (JDAM) Technology fitted onto a bomb or missile that allows flight or ground crews to guide the weapon to its target.

Joint Standoff Weapon (JSOW) Bomb that flies on its own and hits targets accurately.

low observable (LO) features Technologies that make a B-2 difficult to detect or almost invisible.

NATO The North Atlantic Treaty Organization, which consists of North American and European countries that have decided to defend each other and share air force bases around the globe.

nuclear weapons Bombs or missiles containing radioactive materials that explode with great force.

paradigm An outstanding or typical example.

payload A plane's weapons.

prototype An original model.

simulate To practice by re-creating real conditions as precisely as possible.

smart bomb A bomb that is guided (usually by satellite or computer) to hit its target accurately.

sortie A mission flown by a plane.

stealth The ability to be nearly undetectable.

synthetic aperture radar A type of radar that sends out a small signal that is harder to detect than conventional radar.

Taliban An extreme Islamic group that formerly ruled Afghanistan and supported Al Qaeda and Osama bin Laden.

wing An air force term for a group of planes, pilots, and crew who work at a specific air force base.

yaw To deviate wildly from a set path in a left-to-right motion.

FOR MORE INFORMATION

Air Combat Command
Office of Public Affairs
115 Thompson Street, Suite 211
Langley AFB, VA 23665-1987
(757) 764-5007

Federation of American Scientists
1717 K Street NW, Suite 209
Washington, DC 20036
(202)546-3300
Web site: http://www.fas.org/index.html

Office of the Secretary of Defense (Public Affairs)
1400 Defense Pentagon, Room 3A750
Washington, DC 20301-1400
(703) 697-5737
Web site: http://www.defenselink.mil

United States Air Force
Public Affairs Resource Library
1690 Air Force Pentagon
Washington, DC 20330-1690
Web site: http://www.af.mil

Web Sites

Due to the changing nature of Internet links, the Rosen Publishing Group, Inc., has developed an online list of Web sites related to the subject of this book. This site is updated regularly. Please use this link to access the list:

http://www.rosenlinks.com/usw/b2sp/

FOR FURTHER READING

Chant, Christopher, and Michael J. Taylor. *The Role of the Fighter and Bomber*. Broomall, PA: Chelsea House, 2000.

Grant, Rebecca. *The B-2 Goes to War*. Arlington, VA: IRIS Press, 2001.

Pace, Steve. *B-2 Spirit: The Most Capable War Machine on the Planet*. New York: McGraw-Hill, 1999.

Schleifer, Jay. *Bomber Planes*. Mankato, MN: Capstone Press. 1996.

Sweetman, Bill. *Stealth Bombers: The B-2 Spirits*. Mankato, MN: Capstone Press, 2001.

BIBLIOGRAPHY

The Aircraft Gallery. "Northrop Grumman B-2A Spirit." 1997–2000. Retrieved March 2, 2002 (http://www.geocities.com/sunflare98/planes/b-2/).

Ashworth, Brett. "Pilot First to Hit 1,000 Flying-Hour Milestone in B-2." *Air Force News*, May 27, 1999. Retrieved March 5, 2002 (http://www.af.mil/news/May1999/n19990527_991067.html).

"B-2 Stealth Bomber: The Home of the Beast." Retrieved March 9, 2002 (http://www.abs.net/~maddock/LO/b2a_spirit.html).

BBC News. "Guide to Military Strength." Retrieved March 2, 2002 (http://news.bbc.co.uk/hi/english/world/americas/newsid_1557000/1557140.stm#stealth).

CNN.com. "In Depth Special: War on Terror." Retrieved March 3, 2002 (http://www.cnn.com/SPECIALS/2001/trade.center/retal.section.html).

Edwards Air Force Base. "B-2 Spirit." Retrieved March 3, 2002 (http://www.edwards.af.mil/articles98/docs_html/splash/jan98/cover/b2_spirit.html).

Federation of American Scientists. "United States Nuclear Forces: B-2 Spirit." Retrieved March 9, 2002 (http://www.fas.org/nuke/guide/usa/bomber/b-2.htm).

Global Security.org. "B-2 Spirit." Retrieved March 2, 2002 (http://www.globalsecurity.org/wmd/systems/b-2.htm).

Hastings, David. "Target Lock: The Military Aviation E-Zine." Retrieved March 3, 2002 (http://users.ox.ac.uk/~daveh/Military/).

Katzaman, Jim. "Stealth Works, Says Wing Commander." *Air Force News*, May 6, 1999. Retrieved March 3, 2002 (http://www.af.mil/news/May1999/n19990506_990888.html).

Klemens, Susan M. "Mission Invisible." Discovery Online. 1998. Retrieved March 4, 2002 (http://www.discovery.com/area/ technology/b2/b2.html).

Northrop Grumman. "United States Air Force's B-2 Spirit." 2001. Retrieved March 5, 2002 (http://www.iss.northgrum.com/ products/usaf_products/b2/b2.html).

Oliveri, Frank. "The Spirit of Missouri." *Air Force Magazine*, April 1994, Vol. 74, No. 4. Retrieved March 5, 2002 (http://www.afa.org/ magazine/April1994/0494spiri.html).

Tirpak, John A. "With Stealth in the Balkans." *Air Force Magazine*, October 1999, Vol. 82, No. 10. Retrieved March 5, 2002 (http://www.afa.org/magazine/Oct1999/1099stealth.html).

Tirpak, John A. "With the First B-2 Squadron." *Air Force Magazine*, April 1996, Vol. 79, No. 4. Retrieved March 5, 2002 (http://www.afa.org/magazine/April1996/0496witht.html).

United States Air Force Fact Sheet. "B-2 Spirit." Retrieved March 7, 2002 (http://www.af.mil/news/factsheets/B_2_Spirit.html).

Whiteman Air Force Base. Retrieved March 2, 2002 (http://www.whiteman.af.mil/home.htm).

INDEX

CREDITS

About the Author

E. E. Basmadjian is a freelance journalist.

Photo Credits

Cover © Aero Graphics, Inc./Corbis; pp. 4, 14, 34 © David Halford; p. 5 © Lee Snider/Corbis; pp. 7, 16–17, 26 © AFP/Corbis; pp. 8, 19, 23, 31 © AP/Wide World Photos; pp. 10, 12 © U.S. Air Force; p. 22 © Bettmann/Corbis; p. 25 © Roger Ressmeyer/Corbis; p. 27 © Corbis; p. 37 © Reuters NewMedia, Inc./Corbis.

Layout and Design

Thomas Forget

Editor

Annie Sommers